HEART
AND
SOUL

Shiela Y. Harris

Copyright © 2014

ISBN-13: 978-0967931289
ISBN-10: 0967931282

Introduction

As an indie writer and poet I have a vivid awareness of my life's events. My poetry oftentimes reflects these events and is expressed through sound, and rhythmic language choices, so as to evoke an emotional response from my readers.

Poetry is known to employ meter and rhyme, but because of its numerous styles and terminology over centuries this is by no means a necessary or required technique. Poetry is an ancient form that has gone through numerous and drastic reinventions over time. The very nature of poetry is an authentic and individual genre of expression.

My mother often reminds me that very early in my life I had a pencil in my hand and as far back as I can remember writing has been a passion. From love letters to teen boys, Sunday school plays and skits, newsletters, writing interests of young love; to creating my own greeting cards so I could express my true and personal feelings.

This is truly inspired from my *heart* and *soul* as each poem expresses varied emotions of passion, pain and placidity for their moment in time, which helps me emotionally catalogue various segments of my life in a literary perspective.

TABLE OF CONTENT

TABLE OF CONTENT

INVINCIBLE WOMAN

They say I am *invincible*
Because I do not break under pressure
They say I am *unbeatable*
Because I never give up
They say I am unconquerable
Because I am an army of one
They say I am *unshakeable*
Because I am not easily surprised
They say I am *indomitable*
Because of my strength
The say I am *impregnable*
Because I am divinely protected
They say I am *unassailable*
Because I am sure of my self-worth
They say I am *insuperable*
Because I do not run from challenges
They say I am *delectable*
Because I am insatiable to men
I am *incredible*
Because I am an *invincible* woman

<u>GOD'S WOMAN</u>

Made in the image of God
God's woman

Taken from the side of man
To work alongside of man
God's woman

Adorned with beauty,
Sensitivity and strength
God's woman

Mothers, wives
Teaches and preachers
Prophets and business persons and more
God's woman

Created to praise
And intimately worship Him
God's Woman

IT

Life teaches us that we can be frail and apt to stumble and completely fall before we can stand erect again.

It matters not the title or position, because we were born into sin and iniquity the propensity for all of us to fall is there, no matter how spiritual we think we are we just need our, "it."

Our weaknesses are the problem. We all have an "it," and if we do not keep "it" under subjection, continuously seeking to and therefore walking in deliverance, empowered by the Spirit of God our "it" may over take us weakening and confusing our flesh and the simple ability to choose right over wrong.

My real concern is, no matter where I am in life if I should stumble over "it," will there be someone there not to cover me in the error of "it", but to still love me, nurture and mentor me back into right standing with God.

I have made choices that had nothing to do with "flesh" or "sin" or an "it"; it was simply what God needed me to do at the time.

Friends, how many do we have? Friends have dropped like flies, love has vanished for something that was not an "it" issue. So what would happen if I should stumble and fall over an "it?"

With this thought, I pray God will put genuine "friends" and "acquaintances" in my life that will be there for "me" even if "IT" should arise. Shalom

Heaven

I wonder what you're doing there in heaven.
I wonder if you ever think of me.
I know that you are happy there in heaven
I know that I will see,
I know that we will be
living there with God eternally.

I know that there's no sickness there in heaven.
But Oh my God - to worship at His feet.
No pain or sadness ever there in heaven.
I know that you are well,
The stories you will tell
Living there with God eternally.

Have you met your mom and brother there in heaven
Other friends and other family
Moms mind is free and Frankie's body made whole
I know that they are well
No more sickness to compel
and the Face of Jesus now you all can see.

Get a Job

I understand it's a jungle out there
And life is a race you cannot beat
But GR will not do my friend
If you want to be with me
(Get a job)

You're not disabled
Nor deaf or dumb
You walk upright on two feet
Hard work builds character and
And if you want to be with me
(Get a job)

Don't do drugs
Please don't smoke
Don't need a man that tweaks
Abled bodied man of valor
And if you want to be with me
(Get a job)

Extravagant clothes and diamond rings
Are not a necessity
Good conversation and quality time
And monogamy is a must you see
If you want to be with me
(Get a job)

Liberal, intense, loyal and loving
Is what you can expect from me
Walking upright man of God
Is what you'll have to be
If you want to be with me
(Get a job)

If I Could...
(Song to God)

If I could somehow live without life's pain –
I would
If I could go from day to day without stress or strain –
I would
If every day could be sunshine could I do without the rain
I know I could not live;
and I never want to live
without you –
God not without you

Would I live, if I could without lack or need –
I would
If I could live I would in perfect harmony –
I would
I know nothing's impossible or too hard for God
I know I could not live;
and I never want to live
without you –
God not without you.

<u>Some Things My Mom Taught Me</u>

Acknowledge God daily
So others see the God in you
Strive to be different
Make an effort to excel
Do not try to live up to others expectations of you
Walk confidently so others accept who you are
Do not be ashamed of your successes or gifting
Do not hide your abilities or achievements
Do not make light of, or excuses for your achievements
Do what pleases you and makes you happy as long
As it's lawful spiritually and naturally
Avoid dwelling on the negative thoughts from others of you
Embrace your individuality and uniqueness
Man cannot limit you if God is elevating you
Be gracious and watchful
Do not waste time getting even
Spend your time enjoying life
God's judgment will be sufficient
In all your ways acknowledge Him and
He shall direct thy path.

WHY SHOULD I ALLOW YOU
<u>TO TAKE CHANCES WITH MY LIFE?</u>

Marriage should be honored by all, and the marriage bed kept pure, for God will judge the adulterer and all the sexually immoral. Heb. 13:14

Why should I allow you to take chances with my life?
I never had STD's until I married you.
If you loved me you would protect me, and you do not protect
Having unprotected sex with others and you are married to me.
Why are we always told to stay in the marriage because …
God does not honor divorce.
It is also true He does not honor adultery or
Infidelity either but that never comes up in "counseling".
All I hear is what "I should do" to save the marriage and I did
Nothing to cause the problems…
Does anyone care how I feel, what this has done to me?
Why is it my responsibility to keep peace and keep you happy
So you will not stray like a dog in heat?
Marriage is a partnership by which we both vowed
To respect and love one another
To be truthful there is nothing left for me to try and save.
Who actually benefits from all this hard work on MY part?
You crawl between the sheets and I cringe because I…
Am sleeping with everyone you've slept with; and
Sleeping with who they are sleeping with or slept with
I exhale when you're done and realize more and more this is not
How I want to spend the rest of my life…wondering

How will I know...take your word?
I took your word when we gave our vows.
Why should I allow myself to take chances
Of contracting HIV AIDS,
Herpes, Syphilis, Gonorrhea (two of these are death sentences?)
I love me and my life, my family and my children and I love you.
It is surely not because I could not attract and sleep with
another...I chose not to.
Why? Because I love you and I honored you and what
God gave us as a couple.
My intimacy was reserved for you...a lifetime commitment.
Oh! Now you want forgiveness? You got that ... I will give you that.
But! I refuse to live the rest of my days with you
Wondering if you are faithful
How will I know? I already gave you all of me,
My loyalty, love, life, body
And you walked all over that.
Just threw caution to the wind.
Did you ever think of the consequences or did you really care?
But what you won't have is my life or body
To take chances with anymore.
I will no longer allow you to take chances with my life

CHRISTMAS TIME

Christmas should be a happy time joyous for you and for me
But there's not much happiness for those living on the streets
We have our gifts and toys and trees,
and festive family dinner spreads
But what about the homeless child,
Who'd be satisfied with a morsel of bread?

Christmas brings joy and cheer to all who have, no doubt
Our lavish gifts and decorative trees
and twinkling lights inside and out
But to the child that has no home their fate may be uncertain
We have the power to share God's love to many far and near
All it takes is for us to care enough, to spread his joy and cheer

Christmas can impel selfishness from those who will not see
The thousands of those who receive no food, or toys or even a tree
Yes, we may share a token or give a bag, for a one day treat
But what happens the rest of the year
to relieve hunger and cover bare feet?
Will we continue year end and out to think not of other's tight spot
Usually considered to be the haves or the have not's

Please, look around and you will see no need to look very far
So many people and families we can help to bring a little joy
Are we not our brother's keeper as in Genesis 4:9?
Or will we lie as Cain did – and be cursed, for all time
Are we empty, religious and vain, with a form of godliness?
Displaying God's love as a sign high above in an eagle's nest?
Heart felt Agape love is what all people need to feel and see

Real concern through sacrifice, of all our want and need
The Gift of Christmas is for all mankind to celebrate and enjoy
Make Christmas time – a time of giving
to every man, woman, girl and boy.

SPENDING TIME WITH GOD

When I arise after the sun peaks through and over the clouds
Thinking about the day ahead and all that needs to be done
My thoughts wander and I remember,
"I need to spend some time with God"

And I will right after I cleanse myself,
put on some clothes
and grab a quick bite to eat
For I know spending time is what I'll do
or my day is so incomplete

Turned on the computer let it boot up
so I can see Twitter, Face book and emails
Who is in these rooms today anyone I know on Myspace
Just twelve emails and a few face book remarks I'll quickly read
Write a brief answer and then I will spend time with Thee.

"Father God I..."oh the phone is ringing and it is a business call.
I'11 take it while I sweep the floor and freshen up the walls.
On yes! An order a job to do, God knows just what I need
And yes I must spend some time now
spend time with God, with God you see.

Look at the time how quickly it flies it soon will be past noon
Did I say my prayers when I awake this morning?
My what all did I do?
I'll write an article that's on my mind while I can think.
And then I must take a break so God I can spend time with you.

HEART AND SOUL

My what a revelation as God speaks wisdom through me,
as I pen the words he gives to me with such clarity
It is so wonderful to belong to God to be a child of the King
to have the freedom and the time to honor, thank and talk with
Him as His Glory rises in me.

Oh my! What a powerful song, I am a worshipper you see.
The lyrics are ringing; "Lord you are welcome in this place,"
tears are rolling, running down my cheeks
Oh my spirit cannot quench this thirst,
God how I hunger after thee.
Oh God please forgive me,
I will spend some time with thee.

No longer will I be distracted or rush through days or weeks
Just doing daily things I find important only to me.
I am glad you are a patient and forgiving God
My attention you try to get as I plunge through each day
But I allow unimportant things like calls
and chores to keep me away.

Away from you and all your splendor and Glory ever known
But now I know the substance and continued reward
Of spending time with you God
And time with you alone.

IF OUR EYES COULD SEE

If our eyes could see the things of God
the things that matter most
Not Prada shoes or Oakley frames
but the little girl swinging on the post
And she's out much too late
where can her guardians be?
Bad things happen in the streets at night.
Does anyone miss her not being inside and
are they home to see?

If our eyes would see the unwed mother
whose heart is broke into
She thought the baby she's carrying
whose father she loves too
Would stay by her through thick and thin,
their love was supposed to last
But now she has a child within
and their love is a thing of the past

Don't our eyes see the loneliness
and fear without, within
Is there anyone to care for her
to be a needed friend?
Will she just blend in the world's background
rejected and confused?
They cannot care even for themselves
the baby is a muse

If our eyes could see God's creation
is for all to enjoy
But years of polluted skies and seas
will one day be our void
Unhealthy foods, governments corrupt
using too much energy
our land and seas, rivers and lakes
give up more dead than alive you see
...if our eyes could see.

If our eyes will see a hungry child
their eyes lit with begging and pleading
Please help me the house is filled with people
but no one really caring for me
They eat from trash wherever found and
sleep upon a cold hard ground
Days and nights wandering round
and round oh where might help be...
if our eyes will see...

If our eyes could see above our need and greed
caring only for ourselves
We see things that are so sad and we would like to but...
won't someone come and help
We have our problems large and small
this has to be for someone else ...
if our eyes could see.

As time passes on don't be fooled my friends
with prayer calloused knees
God is looking for the pure in heart
and those with eyes that can see

THE QUIET OF NIGHT

It is amazing how the glow of the moon light
and twinkling stars are enough to light our way
The nightfall sonnets are so different from the days
rustling sounds of people moving and car engines humming.

The quiet of night has no songs of birds or windblown trees
yet in its quietness if you listen,
you can hear the stillness of the wind
moving across the pane of your window
and a dog barking in the distance

Laying quietly your thoughts may be reminiscent
of events joyful and sad
while reflecting on today's events and of days past
Knowing the stillness can bring peace or fear
and when thoughts of sadness, loneliness or fear arise
we remember the peace and promises the WORD provides.

The quiet of night can give solace and intimacy with the creator
not afforded during a raucous day.
Use this to your advantage while gazing at
the moon and its many faces, the
Twinkling light of the stars dancing
because it is often God speaks, in the
quiet of night.

<u>OH TO WORSHIP</u>

Worship is a lifestyle not a sonnet with a rhyme
Worship is relationship with God so gloriously divine
Worship is not just a good feeling or emotion.
Even though one may weep
Worship is entering in, bowed down at the master's feet.

Worship cannot be created or conjured at a whim
True Worship is to God alone as water to a stream
A diadem and accolades given purely to the King
God inhabits the praises of His people but worship He esteems

Man made a little lower than the Angels
in the image of his creator
And only men can Worship God from desert to the shore.
Formed from the dust of the earth Created to worship thee
Oh to Worship God in all His splendor and majesty

Give unto the LORD the glory due unto his name;
The more you give true worship the more your life sustain
Worship the LORD in the beauty of holiness
with all that is within you.
God is spirit, and those who worship him
must worship Him, in spirit and in truth

THE WEIGHT OF LIFE

Life is unpredictable like the end to a book
even though its pages unfold daily
We travel its roads with eventful expectations
to sometimes find the unexpected
Things tugging at our hearts and minds –
as weights much too heavy to carry
Many minds silently question
"What is the meaning of life,"
while others think,
"What does this mean for my life?" ...
Today's episodes, yesterday's quandaries.

We step into and out of life from day to day,
carrying unnecessary weight, but
how do we know this?
The weight has been a burden for a long time now.
I dare not release it for it must
have some definitive meaning to my existence.
Why if I release it now, I will never discover its purpose.

Though cumbersome and heavy,
I've become accustomed to it, the weight.
Arise with it, carry it through the day
and retire with it at days end.
Surely God has some purpose for this
no matter how heavy it is.
When and if I should release it,
what would I do without it then?

You say, "Give it to Jesus" and leave it with Him,
what will He do with it?
I have done this so many times o'er but it just returns.
You see it is my burden,
a weight designed particularly for me.
Often it returns more cumbersome
than prior times before.

The weights of life, will I ever be able to release them?
God knows I am a pessimist and never optimistic.
As a cynic I never expect better,
therefore guarding against disappointments
My life is a continuous episode of weights
bearing down like granite rock
A prisoner of my own thoughts,
a victim of a fate I choose in the weight of life

<u>GONE MUCH TO SOON</u>

When you entered you'd light up the room
with your antique humor and dazzling shoes
People-person you were everyone gravitating
and hanging on to your every word
Gone Much Too Soon

Your wit and wisdom
Often none could compare
And a hint of arrogance usually in the air
Could communicate most subjects
Mind filled to the brim
With knowledge of both the now and then
Gone Much Too Soon

Tried to keep your essence in all things there
Clothes, shoes, hats, in all things you wear
Time fades away and eventually memories
Fill space and air - - but why -- you then?
Of all those that could be retracted
All those good and bad surely
There were others absence that would not
Make many hearts sad
Gone Much Too Soon

Talents, there were many most birthed before their time
Talent that needed to be channeled and challenged
To be enjoyed and pondered by those
That are left behind - you see
You are Gone Much too Soon

What about the seventy years life span
Promised to the righteous man?
And how about the prophesies regarding your health
Did not they still stand?
Your work here could not have been finished
There is still so much to do so many to mentor
Your heart had the beat of ministry
You Are Gone Much Too Soon

GONE BUT NOT FORGOTTEN

Two years have come and gone so quickly
My how the time flies
It seems it was just yesterday
For the last time you closed your eyes

You will never know how much you're missed
By people everywhere
Acquaintances, family and friends
People far and near

Tyree & Corey say all the time
How much they miss you too
How you ran things like a tight ship
So the excellence of God shined through

You're gone from this earth to live with God
My how glorious that must be
To sit at the feet of Jesus
From now through eternity

Gone but not forgotten
Your legacy lives on
Especially through your
Teaching, and music and in song

<u>HEAVEN'S BEST</u>

While you here with us on earth
You made everyone smile
Pressed untiringly in kingdom work
Perfection was your style

Your legacy will be remembered
Through music and ministry
Your love of life was an endearment
To all who were able to see

Your love will always be treasured
God knew you would stand His tests
Your faithfulness cannot be measured
You are one of Heaven's Best

BUTTERFLY

The butterfly is beautiful
And it's lovely colored wings
It usually emerges from a cocoon
During the height of Spring

How marvelous the transformation
How glorious the sight
When the morph from larva
Into a winged flight

An array of colors and species
A rainbow does not compare
When the colors of their wings
Reflect the daylight so fair

When I see Jesus
That's how it will be
Changing from mortal
To immortality

<u>MY PRAYER</u>

My prayer today is as we sit in our churches
and host revivals and musicals; summits
and celebrations attended greatly by the saved;
we also focus on equipping us
as we seek a deeper discernment
and concern
for our hurting and spiritually lost young people
whose lives are being wasted and destroyed
because they see no way out.

I also pray we concentrate a little more on Kingdom Agenda
(rather than celebrating each other)
And continue neglecting the true cause for Christ

From now through eternity
Let's see those among us
(who are silently crying for help)
and go outside the walls and weekly traditions
using our God given power to influence LIFE.

WHO THE SON SETS FREE
<u>IS FREE INDEED</u>

Rescued from my destruction
Freed from all my sin
Delivered from my habit
Since I gave my life to Him
The invincible the immortal
The invisible the only God
Who the Son sets free, is free indeed

Walking with no direction
My way is hard to see
The heavy weight of rejection
With loneliness and defeat
The invincible the immortal
The invisible the only God
Who the Son sets free, is free indeed

<u>MY NEED OF YOU</u>

My need of you is not to complete me
But to complement our lives as we are one
Not to make me over to meet other's expectations
But to intensify the woman I've become

Our walk together speaks volumes of love
Expressing our loyalty during ebbs and tides
Never allowing anything or anyone to shove
Protecting each other from the world's snares

My need of you is not to lose myself
In a world that voids validating me
Hiding my perfect imperfections
Shading feminine uniqueness and quality

Love is a miracle of intertwining differences
A pair – a species created to be
Soul mates of mere flesh and bone
Bonding their lives for all too see

I need from you and you need from me
Endless love and timeless moments
Because what God brings together
Should last all eternity.

SETH
Great Grandson Born: March 26, 2014

Third son born to Adam and Eve
Some believe as an anointed compensation for Abel
Nourished and fed through your mother's womb
Kicking and flaying hands on the table.

My Great Grandson born healthy and strong
Destined to be used of God
Born to a family of orators and scholars
Athletes, musicians which road will you trod?

Lungs are strong and alert you are
Kicking and ready to thrive
Long legs, hands, and fingers and toes
Waving wildly in the air to make your birth known.

A son to your mother and father
A gift from God what a blessing you are
Grandson, cousin and nephew to others
Praying your life will take you far.

From the moment you were conceived
I've prayed fervently for you
For God to stay the hand of Satan
As His assigned Angels cover you too

Make your mark on the pillars of society
As you walk the road less traveled
May in this world wise you will be
And God's goodness and mercy follow
You all the days of your life!

THE GIANT SEQUOIA TREE

The tallest tree in the world, the largest tree on earth
Amongst crescent meadows and Tokopah Falls
Three-thousand and Two-Hundred years old;
Two hundred and forty seven feet tall

Gazing up the sunlight trickles down through the branches
Treetops seem like giant bean stalks piercing the sky
Beside them we look like ants on a trail
Wondering how anything can stand that high

A tunnel cut through a felled giant sequoia tree
Surrounded by mighty waterfalls and granite cliffs
Glimpse the Beautiful view atop Morrow rock
Four-hundred steps to the top.

The landscape testifies to nature's size and beauty
With unimaginable diversity
With huge mountains, rugged foothills, deep canyons
All engulfed by the world's largest trees

How great is our God someone ask
A poet said no poem is as lovely as a tree
He's the creator of all we see
Including the giant sequoia tree.

A SERVANT'S QUARTERS

(Written when my Aunt Vivian was celebrating 30 years as Church Clerk in 1980)

There is a place where I am told
the streets are paved with gold
They say the gates are made of pearl
and waters run deep and cold

Angelic choirs sing praises to their King
It is a place reserved for those
Who've served their master well
It is said there is no dying there
or crying in this place so fair

Maybe a limousine and flowers
should line your way
Or golden gems be given to you this day
But instead, many who love you dear
have gathered here to say
"Thank You," for your years of service
in their own special way

But in this place that is so fair
awaits for you and me
A special honor no man can give,
just Jesus Christ our King

And so we have no rubies,
diamonds or gems to give
You must wait to receive for your servant's crown
when it's all over here

A place where you shall see the glory
of our savior's face
A place that waits for you in glory
In your servants quarters there

HAVE YOU EVER

Have you ever heard a Blue Bird cry
Have you ever seen a cloudless sky
Have you ever walked a mile for ice cream

Have you ever seen the break of day
Have you ever been to outer space
Have you ever smelled the fragrance of new spring

My spirit leaped within itself
Felt a love I've never, ever felt
Today I felt my heart skip a beat

I have never seen the bottom of the sea
Never been with you or you with me
But today I heard my heart skip a beat

www.ingramcontent.com/pod-product-compliance
Lightning Source LLC
Chambersburg PA
CBHW061758040426
42447CB00011B/2366